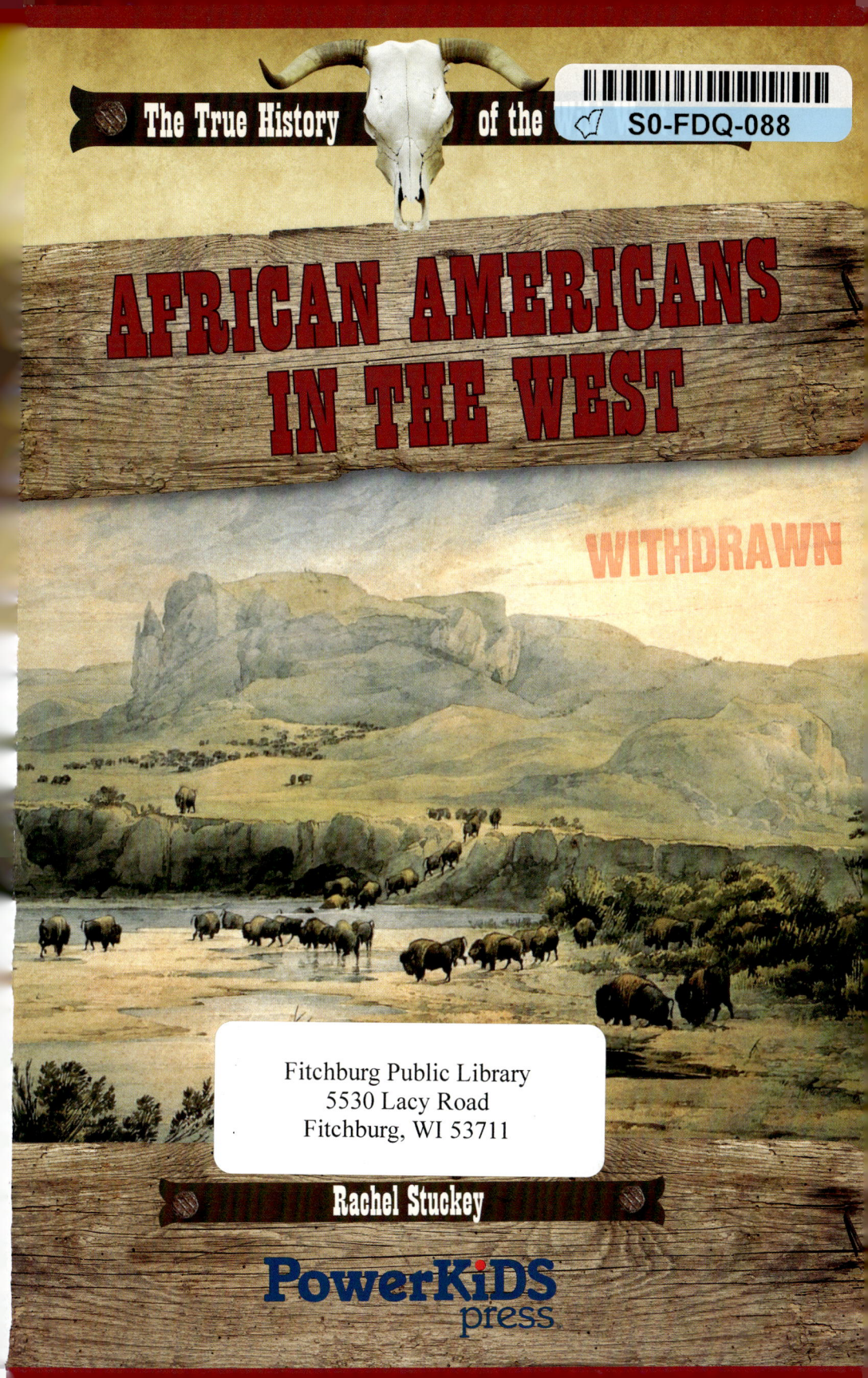

The True History of the
AFRICAN AMERICANS IN THE WEST

Rachel Stuckey

PowerKiDS press

Published in 2016 by **The Rosen Publishing Group, Inc.**
29 East 21st Street, New York, NY 10010

Copyright © 2016 by The Rosen Publishing Group, Inc.

All rights reserved. No part of this book may be reproduced in any form without permission in writing from the publisher, except by a reviewer.

Developed and produced for Rosen by BlueAppleWorks Inc.

Art Director: T.J. Choleva
Managing Editor for BlueAppleWorks: Melissa McClellan
Designer: Joshua Avramson
Photo Research: Jane Reid
Editor: Marcia Abramson

Illustration & Photo Credits: Cover, p. 10, 13, 14, 19 Carlyn Iverson; title page Karl Bodmer/Public Domain; cover, title page, back cover (skull) Jim Parkin/Shutterstock; cover, title page (wood) Dagmara_K/Shutterstock; back cover background homydesign/Shutterstock; background siro46/Shutterstock; chapter intro backgrounds rangizzz/Shutterstock; p. 4 Julian Scott/Public Domain; p. 6 Charles Marion Russell/Public Domain; p. 8-9, 22-23 U.S. National Archives and Records Administration/Public Domain; p. 9, 20, 22 Public Domain; p. 16 Library of Congress Prints and Photographs Division/Public Domain; p. 18-19 Alfred Jacob Miller/Public Domain; p. 24 Frederic Remington/Public Domain; p. 26 Thomas Hill/Public Domain; p. 28 Great Northern Railway/Public Domain; p. 28 inset Jack Delano/Library of Congress/Public Domain

Cataloging-in-Publication-Data

Stuckey, Rachel.
African Americans in the west / by Rachel Stuckey.
p. cm. — (The true history of the Wild West)
Includes index.
ISBN 978-1-4994-1172-0 (pbk.)
ISBN 978-1-4994-1202-4 (6 pack)
ISBN 978-1-4994-1193-5 (library binding)
1. African Americans — West (U.S.) — History — Juvenile literature.
2. Frontier and pioneer life — West (U.S.) — Juvenile literature.
I. Stuckey, Rachel II. Title.
E185.925 S78 2016
978'.00496073—d23

Manufactured in the United States of America

CPSIA Compliance Information: Batch #WS15PK
For Further Information contact: Rosen Publishing, New York, New York at 1-800-237-9932

CONTENTS

Chapter 1
Leaving the South for the West 5

Chapter 2
Buffalo Soldiers 7

Chapter 3
Mighty Cowboys 11

Chapter 4
In the Midst of It All 17

Chapter 5
Towards the Modern Era 25

Glossary 30

More Information 31

Index 32

The South waved the white flag of surrender in 1865. After that, ex-slaves could travel freely.

Leaving the South for the West

The Civil War, which lasted from 1861 to 1865, is an important time in American history. President Abraham Lincoln opposed slavery and did not want new states and territories to make slavery legal. In 1861, the slave states **seceded** from the United States and formed the Confederate States of America. Soon the **Union** and the **Confederacy** were at war. More Americans died in the Civil War than in any other war.

After the war, society in both the North and the South was still racially prejudiced. So many African Americans traveled west for new opportunities. They claimed land and became farmers, ranchers, and even gold and silver prospectors. Those who went west even founded their own towns on the frontier, such as Nicodemus in Kansas, Dearfield in Colorado, Langston City and Boley in Oklahoma, and Allensworth in California.

Buffalo were smart, fast, and tricky. This earned the respect of Native Americans.

Buffalo Soldiers

After the Civil War, the United States Congress established the first all-African American peacetime **regiments**. Many African Americans served in the Union army during the Civil War. Free men from the North were allowed to join the army for the first time during the war. The Union army also allowed the slaves they freed to join the army. After the war, many more former slaves joined the army. It was a great opportunity for them to leave the South.

As Americans moved west, the U.S. Army went west to defend the frontier. Four regiments of African American soldiers were sent west. There were many **skirmishes** and battles on the **Great Plains** with both Native Americans and Mexicans. The Native Americans called the all-African American regiments Buffalo Soldiers. The nickname was a compliment from the Native Americans. Buffalo were strong and fast and very difficult to hunt.

Buffalo Soldiers first served in the West, then in every U.S. war through the 1950s. They were known for their skill and bravery.

Four regiments of Buffalo Soldiers served on the frontier. There were two infantry units and two **cavalry** units. These regiments fought in conflicts against Native Americans and Mexicans. Like the rest of the army, the Buffalo Soldiers had many jobs on the frontier. They also helped to build roads and protected the people who delivered the U.S. mail. When there were conflicts between groups of ranchers, the Buffalo Soldiers helped to stop the fighting.

Henry Ossian Flipper

White officers usually commanded the Buffalo Soldiers, but there were some African American officers. Lieutenant Henry Ossian Flipper was a former slave who graduated from West Point Military Academy in 1871. He was respected by his men and by his commanding officer because of his military skills. Lt. Flipper still faced prejudice and eventually he had to leave the army. He worked as an engineer and then as assistant to the U.S. Secretary of the Interior.

African American cowboys often had to do the toughest tasks, but they still faced less discrimination than in the rest of the country.

Mighty Cowboys

The life of a cowboy was hard work. Good **ranch** hands had to ride a horse well, even through a cattle **stampede**. Cowboys also had to round up and rope cattle. In **cattle drives**, cowboys would move a herd of cattle up to 1,000 miles (1,609 km). Cowboys also had to be able to shoot a rifle to help protect the cattle from **rustlers**.

In Hollywood Westerns, the cowboys are usually white movie stars. But one out of every four cowboys on the western frontier was African American. There were also many Native American cowboys, and about one third of cowboys were Mexican. There were even cowgirls. Not quite what you see in the movies!

Cowboys spent most of their time on the **range** where skills were more important than anything else. When cowboys went to town, it didn't matter if they were African American or Hispanic or Native American, as long as they had money to spend!

Fact Check - TRUTH OR MYTH?

MYTH: All cowboys were gunslingers.

TRUTH OR MYTH? This is a myth. Guns were necessary on the frontier, but not as much as we think. Gun control laws were much stricter than today. Guns were not allowed in most towns and murder rates were very low. **Six-shooters** were heavy and not very accurate. Cowboys carried rifles and shotguns to protect themselves and the cattle from mountain lions and the occasional thief. Cowboys usually paid a toll or fee to drive their cattle through Native American territory—they didn't have gun battles!

Bose Ikart

Bose Ikart was a true cowboy. Ikart was born a slave in Mississippi in the 1840s. The family that owned him moved to Texas and Ikart grew up learning the skills of a ranch hand. After the Civil War, he worked for Charles Goodnight, one of the most famous ranchers in Texas. Ikart worked cattle drives from Texas to Montana for Goodnight. Ikart was so well respected and trusted that Goodnight put him in charge of carrying the money on the cattle drives. In 1869, Ikart retired from ranching and became a farmer in Texas.

Nat Love

Nat Love was born a slave in 1854. When the Civil War ended, Love's father tried to start a farm, but he died soon after. So as a teenager, Love headed west. He found work at a ranch in Kansas and learned the skills of a cowboy quickly. At the age of 22 he proved his skills by winning the Fourth of July rodeo in the town of Deadwood in the Dakota Territory. He impressed the crowd so much, they started to call him Deadwood Dick after a character in a Wild West **dime novel**.

In 1907, Love published a book about his life. He wrote about herding cattle and his adventures riding through stampedes, playing in card games, and surviving gunfights. Like other cowboys who wrote books about the Wild West, Love included many tall tales. His stories are very entertaining but not always true!

Bulldogging Bill Pickett

Bill Pickett was born in Texas in 1870. He's the most famous African American cowboy in history. His father was a former slave and his mother was Native American. Pickett was a ranch hand at a very young age. He soon started performing cowboy skills at local fairs. He was a trick-roper and bull rider. He even invented a rodeo trick called **bulldogging**. Bulldogging is now called **steer wrestling** and still part of rodeos today.

In 1907, he joined the Miller Brothers' 101 Ranch Wild West Show. The show traveled all over the country as well as Canada, Mexico,

Tough Cowboy Glory

Fifty years after his death in 1932, Bill Pickett was the first African American inducted into the Cowboy Hall of Fame in Oklahoma. He is also in the Pro Rodeo Hall of Fame. In 1994, the U.S. Postal Service honored Pickett with a stamp in the Legends of the West series.

Fact Check - TRUTH OR MYTH?

MYTH: Gunslingers were fancy shooters.

TRUTH OR MYTH? This is a myth. Gunslingers were the best shooters around, but the idea that the cowboys, outlaws, and sheriffs known as gunslingers were fancy shooters comes from books and movies. Drawing and shooting quickly is not easy to do. It's actually impossible to shoot accurately from the hip. It's also very unlikely that anyone could shoot two guns well at the same time. Even carrying two six-shooters was uncommon. Carrying one four-pound (1.8 kg) pistol was enough!

South America, and England. Pickett also acted in movies about the Wild West. He was the star of the 1922 silent film *The Bull-Dogger*. He was a good friend of Will Rogers, the most famous cowboy performer of the day.

Pickett was famous, but he still faced discrimination. He was not allowed to perform in some towns or even Madison Square Garden in New York City because of his race. Sometimes Pickett would say that he was all Native American to be able to perform. And he could not compete against white cowboys in many rodeos.

Like everyone on the frontier, African American kids had lots of chores, but they also had freedom to play and explore.

In the Midst of It All

Not everyone in the Wild West was a cowboy! African Americans lived in many ways on the frontier. Free men and women and escaped slaves traveled to the frontier looking for opportunity. As more settlers moved west, African Americans became storekeepers, innkeepers, doctors, teachers, farmers, and lawmen. But there was also discrimination. Settlers could claim free land to start farms and ranches, or look for gold and silver. In some places, though, there were laws that prevented African American settlers from keeping their claims.

In the early part of the 1800s, African Americans were explorers, fur traders, and pioneers. Jean Baptiste Du Sable was an African American sailor from Haiti who founded the settlement of Eschikagou, which eventually became the city of Chicago. George Washington Bush was an early fur trader and a wealthy Missouri farmer. He later traveled the **Oregon Trail** and helped start Washington state.

Thousands of African Americans traveled the Oregon Trail from the 1830s to 1869.

Moses "Black" Harris

Moses "Black" Harris is one of the most famous pioneers on the Oregon Trail. We don't know where Harris came from, but in the 1820s he joined an expedition up the Missouri River. He worked as a fur trapper in the mountains. Harris could walk great distances alone and was often sent to St. Louis with information from the frontier. He also helped to build Fort Laramie in Wyoming.

Harris worked as a guide on the Oregon Trail. He helped to guide the very first **wagon train** of settlers across the mountains in 1836. In 1844, Harris guided 500 people on the trail to Fort Vancouver, including pioneer George Washington Bush and his family. More than once, Harris traveled into the Oregon desert to help guide wagon trains to safety. He died of cholera in 1849.

Another George Washington

George Washington was an African American pioneer of the Pacific Northwest. In 1850, at the age of 32, he traveled to Oregon City with the Cochrans, the white family who raised him. Washington cleared 12 acres of land near the Skookumchuck River, built a cabin, and started farming. Because of racist laws, he was not allowed to claim the land. So the Cochran family claimed 640 acres that included Washington's land. Four years later, the family sold him their entire claim.

When the railroad came in the 1870s, Washington decided to build a town, which eventually became Centralia, Washington. He sold plots of land for a low price and donated land for a church, cemetery, and park. Washington also loaned money so others could start businesses. In 1893, he gave people food during an economic crisis.

Slavery on the Frontier

Many African Americans also traveled west as slaves. Before the Civil War, slavery was legal in Arkansas and Texas and there were many slaves on cotton **plantations** and cattle ranches. While not very common, slavery was also legal for some time in the Utah and the New Mexico Territories. In 1865, all the slaves in the western states and territories were freed.

Lawman Bass Reeves

Bass Reeves was born a slave in Arkansas. He moved to Texas with his owner, who was a sheriff and a legislator. When the Civil War broke out, Reeves ran away to Indian Territory in what is now Oklahoma. He lived there for many years and learned to speak native languages. He became a free man in 1865. He later moved back to Arkansas where he became a farmer and raised a family.

A Slave Explorer

A man named York was part of the Lewis and Clark Corps of Discovery in 1804. York had been a slave of the Clark family his whole life and worked as Captain Clark's manservant. York worked hard and was well respected by the rest of the Corps. He was even allowed to vote on group decisions like the rest of the Corps members. But unlike the rest, he was never paid for his work. York was probably the first African American to travel across the country to the Pacific.

In 1875, the new **U.S. Marshal** heard about Reeves' skills and experience in the Indian Territory. He hired Reeves as a deputy for the Oklahoma Indian Territory. That made Bass Reeves one of the first African American Deputy U.S. Marshals west of the Mississippi River. Reeves spent 30 years as a Deputy U.S. Marshall. He never learned to read or write, but Reeves was well-known for his skills as a detective. Reeves also was an excellent shot. He won 14 gunfights without ever being shot himself. He is also said to have arrested 3,000 criminals. Some people believe that Bass Reeves was the inspiration for the Lone Ranger stories.

Stagecoach Mary

Mary Fields was born in 1832, in a log cabin in Tennessee. She lived as a slave until the end of the Civil War. In 1884, at the age of 52, Fields traveled west to Montana. Fields was a very tall woman who often wore men's clothes. She also smoked cigars, drank whiskey, and carried a pistol under her apron. She worked for a convent school, started a restaurant, and ran a laundry. She also drove a **stagecoach**, which is how she got her name.

Mail carriers like Stagecoach Mary faced danger from both thieves and wild animals. Buffalo Soldiers often escorted them.

At the age of 60, Stagecoach Mary was hired by the United States Postal Service. She got the job because she could hitch a team of horses to the stagecoach the fastest. She drove her stagecoach all across the dangerous Montana territory to deliver the mail. She was the first African-American woman to deliver the mail. Also, she was only the second woman to work for the USPS. She lived out her life as an honored citizen of Cascade, Montana. When her house burned down in 1912, people of the town rebuilt it. Stagecoach Mary often had free meals at the town's hotel restaurant, too.

Stagecoaches and many other aspects of the Wild West vanished with the arrival of the railroad.

Towards the Modern Era

In the early 1800s, explorers, fur traders, pioneers, and prospectors pushed the frontier further and further west. The first explorers and fur traders traveled by canoe and horseback and often on foot. They found the way for early pioneers who traveled in wagon trains. Until the 1860s, traveling from the east to the west took four months.

After the Civil War, the first railroads were completed. This made it much easier for people to travel to the west. More people traveled west and they built towns and cities. In 1890, the government announced that the frontier was gone and all the parts of the country had been settled.

Even though they still faced discrimination, the western frontier had been a place of opportunity for African Americans. But as the west became more settled, African Americans began to face the same unfair laws and attitudes they did back east.

The Iron Horse

The first American railroads were built in the 1830s in the eastern states. It took many more years to start building **transcontinental** railroads. The first train that went all the way to California was the Pacific Railroad, completed in 1869. Twenty years later, there were thousands of miles of railroad throughout the west. Many cattle drives, wagon trains, and stagecoaches were replaced by the railroad, or the **Iron Horse**. Travel and business were much easier on a train. The towns built along the railroads quickly turned into cities. The growth of the railroad changed the Wild West forever. The railroads may have ended the opportunities

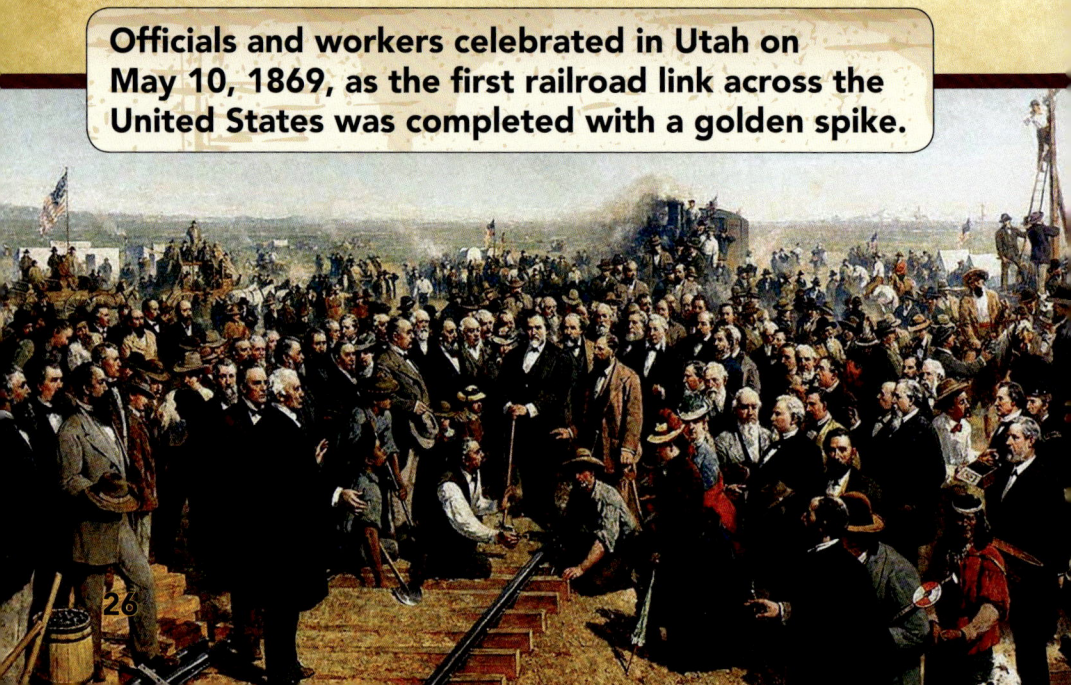

Officials and workers celebrated in Utah on May 10, 1869, as the first railroad link across the United States was completed with a golden spike.

for African Americans to become cowboys and farmers and gold miners in the West. But train travel also created a new opportunity. After the Civil War and the end of slavery, former slaves and other African Americans found paid work in the brand-new industry of train travel.

Pullman Porters

George Pullman invented the first comfortable sleeper car in 1857, which made traveling long distances on the train easier. After the Civil War, Pullman hired former slaves who had worked as domestic servants. These men became porters on Pullman's train cars. Porters carried luggage, served meals, made up the beds, polished shoes, and did anything else passengers needed. There were also women porters who helped female passengers, like domestic maids.

The Pullman Company only hired African Americans for these jobs. These workers were not very well respected by white passengers. In the racist world after slavery ended, the railway porters were thought of as George Pullman's "boys." It was common to call slaves after their owners, so for a long time, Pullman porters were all called George no matter what their name was.

Pullman porters worked from about 1868 to 1968. As train travel declined, the job ended.

In some ways, the Pullman porters and other railway service jobs show the low status of African Americans after slavery ended.

Even so, a railroad job was steady and paid much better than other jobs open to African Americans at the time. Pullman porters helped build the African American middle class. They traveled the country and helped spread information between different communities. They were able to save money and help build churches and schools in their community. Many famous

African American leaders, such as Supreme Court Justice Thurgood Marshall, were the children of Pullman porters or worked as porters themselves.

Myth and Reality

At the same time that African American pioneers were helping to settle the frontier, people all over the world were dreaming of the Wild West. Even today, most of our favorite stories about the Wild West come from the newspaper stories and dime novels of the day. Many of the stories about people like Billy the Kid or Wild Bill Hickok were exaggerated or even made up. The Wild West quickly became a myth or a legend. The live Wild West shows and then movie Westerns helped to create that legend.

Because of racial prejudice, the stories of African Americans in the Wild West were not told. People such as Moses Harris, Bose Ikart, and Mary Fields did not become part of the legend right away. But they were well known and respected in the real Wild West. These people and so many others played an important role in settling the American West.

Glossary

bulldogging The original name for steer wrestling.

cattle drive Moving a large herd of cattle from one place to a another, usually for sale.

cavalry Soldiers that ride horses.

Confederacy The southern states in the Civil War.

dime novel A cheap popular novel in the 1800s.

Great Plains The large grasslands east of the Rocky Mountains.

Iron Horse A nickname for steam engine trains, which were made of iron.

Oregon Trail The route taken by wagon trains in the American West from Missouri to Oregon.

plantation A large farm where crops are tended by slaves or paid workers who live on the farm.

ranch A large farm where animals such as horses or cattle are raised.

range A large area of open land where animals graze or hunt.

regiments A unit of the army.

rustler A person who rounds up and steals horses or cattle.

seceded Formally withdrew from an organization.

six-shooters A type of handgun that holds six bullets.

skirmish Small, unplanned fighting between two groups.

stagecoach A large, enclosed horse-drawn carriage that carried people.

stampede When a group of animals suddenly run in a panic.

steer wrestling A rodeo event where riders wrestle a steer by grabbing its horns.

transcontinental Something that goes across an entire continent.

Union The northern states in the Civil War.

U.S. Marshal A federal law enforcement officer.

wagon trains A group of covered wagons traveling together.

For More Information

Further Reading

Glaser, Jason. *Buffalo Soldiers and the American West*. Mankato, MN: Capstone Press, 2006.

Hicks, Peter. *You Wouldn't Want to Live in a Wild West Town!* New York, NY: Scholastic, 2013.

Murray, Stuart. *Wild West*. New York, NY: DK Eyewitness Books, 2005.

Schlissel, Lillian. *Black Frontiers: A History of African American Heroes in the Old West*. New York, NY: Simon and Schuster, 2000.

Websites

Due to the changing nature of Internet links, PowerKids Press has developed an online list of websites related to the subject of this book. This site is updated regularly. Please use this link to access the list:
www.powerkidslinks.com/thoww/african

Index

A
Abraham Lincoln 5
Arkansas 20

C
Chicago 17
Civil War 5, 7, 12, 13, 20, 22, 25, 27
Colorado 5
cowboys 10, 11, 12, 13, 15, 27

G
guns 15

I
Indian Territory 20, 21

L
Lewis and Clark 21
Lone Ranger 21

M
Mexico 14, 20
Missouri 17, 18
Montana 12, 22, 23

N
Native Americans 6, 7, 8

O
Oklahoma 5, 14, 20, 21
Oregon 17, 18, 19
Oregon Trail 17, 18

R
railroads 25, 26
rodeo 13, 14

S
slavery 5, 20, 27, 28
soldiers 7

T
Texas 12, 14, 20

U
U.S. Marshals 21
U.S. Postal Service 14

W
Washington (state) 17, 18, 19
women 17, 27
Wyoming 18